Harness the Power of the Ocean

NOBUE HAGIWARA

D0899426

Fulton Books, Inc.
Meadville, PA

Published by Fulton Books 2021

ISBN 978-1-64952-764-6 (paperback)
ISBN 978-1-63710-114-8 (digital)

Printed in the United States of America

In loving memory of my
Nana, Charlotte Dorothea Drettler.
Also inspired by the thoughtful,
Melissa Persinger; the inspirational,
Angie Christianson; and the wise, Yenni
Fuenmayor who all helped me throughout
crisis.
Most of all my patient,
steadfast boyfriend, Konrad
Wesley.
In remembrance of my dentist:
Dr. Kenneth A. Hammon, DDS, kept my smile
smiling bright!

Preface / Introduction

I am first and foremost my papa's daughter. My dad is first-generation Japanese who wears baseball caps and has a beautiful smile when he is feeling well. Due to an eye operation that affected the lens of his eye and attached to the eye muscle, he is seen to have an endearing candlebox eye. (I don't like what poor affect he has as a result of using a specific eye doctor). His right one.

I grow impatient and more stubborn with age, but I get that from both sides of my parents. I am the youngest in the family.

Depression followed me throughout adolescence. Ever since middle school, I was self-conscious about my self-image and always was forceful at expressing myself communicably. In high school, I ended up being the shyest senior superlative. I was absolutely convinced that it kinda fit my personality my senior year of high school as senioritis kicked in.

For a person with little to no direction of what to do with myself and predestined an occupation set, it took a toll on me how I really still was in a shell. I am getting to define myself better through journaling and was always preoccupied with homework. As I wrote more and more and often built up my vocabulary, I managed to gain confidence in writing essays. But I feel at a loss that I think the International Baccalaureate program, although useful at regurgitating essay(s), didn't prepare me for the "real world," let alone college life and what it would be like for me.

I really am not one to keep on arguing on opposing opinion, but what I learned was to respect elders. Trust your professors. Get used to micromanaging—it's just a solid part of life everyone has to face to consistently improve one's self.

I personally learn from experience, and I have demonstrated that I can be a go-getter-Greg type of person underneath it all, being reliable and trendy with a balanced professional lifestyle. Hey, if the shoe fits, wear it.

After I dropped out of college, I sought the help of a psychiatrist by the name of Dr. Stephen Bishop. He diagnosed me, saying that my tendencies to isolate myself and withdraw from my surroundings were in fact why I have schizoaffective disorder.

I would be hospitalized repeatedly over a period of fifteen years. I suffered having moments of psychosis where I could suffer auditory and visual hallucinations, and I would not be able to self-soothe easily with my delusional temperance. The pendulum would swing 180 degrees to catatonia where I would be inactive for long periods of time. It would be difficult to articulate to others what behavior I'm experiencing how I simply felt, eventually feeling anguished and relapsing into depression once again.

My nana had a conch seashell in the bathroom as decor. I asked her why she had a conch shell in the bathroom at the age of five, and she lovingly shared me the pearl of wisdom that I hold true: "If you place the conch shell to your left ear, then you can hear the sound of the ocean."

Harness the power of the ocean.

Under a lot of stressful work conditions, I would be prone to panic attacks that made me resort to alprazolam. I had moments where I caved and tried to commit suicide by overdosing on my antipsychotics four times.

Where there is darkness, hopefully you can find the light at the end of the tunnel.

So living homeless, I went from a self-supporting individual who was always punctual and always reliable. To a person who struggled on a regular basis to endure the homeless shelter. Comitis during the winter of originally reusing AMH as an outlet to have me back on the road to more stability, mentally and physically. Reflecting back, I managed to be housed under the care of the Colorado Crisis Center Unit (CSU) right in my hometown, in Aurora, Colorado.

There I met with a wonderful counselor, Melissa, who helped me find a house through the landlord of the independent housing, Everett G, since I had no income whatsoever. I had medical bills dating back from 2012, which financially crippled me. She was a liaison between therapists and landlord for me.

I received help from the therapist, Yenni, who would spend time to talk with me even when I was a total wreck, when anxiety took control over myself. She taught me methods of self-soothing and was a good listener like the therapist, Angie. Both were excellent in assisting me with referring back on the HALT method (Hungry, Angry, Lonely, Tired [Stressed]) in DBT, from the Health and Wellness classes provided by the CSU unit, and also the classes at AMH.

Over time, the tools provided from the classes alone and the resources of having a roof over my head allowed for me to recoup, reflect, journal, learn a new skill (jewelry making), work continuously on open communications, and communicating were effective.

I felt despair at an all-time high, only getting up to three hours of sleep per night at Comitis. But it kept me warm and was temporary. I stayed there two weeks until I got the housing assistance. Too many people crowded in small confines of the bunk bedded building with homeless individuals such as myself who are struggling without food stamps for a time being, snoring people, phones going off, and background music being played on stereo devices.

Made me wise up fast.

Overall I look back and reassuringly depend on my saying, "Depression is *anger* without motivation."

It might be a well-known saying to those who suffer from mental health, along with their issues on a regular basis.

This compilation of five hundred poems I wrote fervently through keeping journal after journal, notebook after notebook is a way of me expressing creatively my freelance writing skills; to help others who have faced dead ends, trying hard to stay connected and surface up.

It has waves of emotion, feelings, thoughts, and mannerisms that describe the many idiosyncrasies that is *me*.

Tidbit reminds me of the comedy movie starring Amy Adams, *Talladega Nights*.

Not giving away spoilers though.

There's a location in the mountains, on the route going toward Georgetown, that passes by a river running along the side and a bridge dedicated to a victim who was mauled and attacked by a mountain lion. This Puma bridge lets those venturing in the mountains, walking or hiking, along the vast forests to be aware and stay alert for any mountain lions and follow etiquette to make one look massive and scare it.

I want to take a brief moment to pay homage to the bridge and pray for the victim's family. I do.

If I had only eaten corned beef and hash made by my opa, then it would alleviate the Oedipus Rex curse. But then I remembered of Sam's No. 3 Restaurant, which is just as good.

I've gone through an entirety of six pens altogether, maybe eight, writing haikus, sonnets, memories, song lyrics, poetry, to fashion *me* retrospectively.

It is within my hopes that you, as the reader, can sympathize, laugh, or enjoy reading this collection.

Untitled

I buy the cafe press sticker
It's AAFES
cabbage take heed
luggage

Sold the house

up for sale
time to meet w/ Paula Hale

Untitled

I had my last French onion soup
You crucible nest egg
Saints cry of how
The Everly Bros. blessed
My Kiss your face(R)
And you appeared into my
Life crickets chirp out back
As a dark brunette emo
My feeling of a gecko.

Riesling wine (for one)

Close the gate
Open the window
Wash the dishes
A bowl of clam chowder
Let it have a day
Then dish rack dry
You cleaned the fork right
You took the train along the
Plain through Spain, you Spaniard
Thousand island dressing on
A sandwich.

Larisa

Wait on me
"You see three"
Of the good tales
While taking sales
I'm all caught up on duck tales.

Anton Yelchin S Twilight

Gravitate and evaluate
You're comprised
Of no mention lies
Compromised to the core
Then you must soar
Afloat the Eagle's nebula
Gravitate as my muse.

From Peter to Paul, grandma shawl

If you believe well without
Knowing, all the right
Methods of which you're
Forgoing, catch the
Moment you having higher
Rent, with each last cent
We all get heaven sent
Now I'm feelin' spent.

John Krasinski

I hereby consider you as a William C. Hinkley alumni
You've earned a certified Auto Zone tire rotation of 3,001 mileage.
This and more haikus on the way.

Matt Damon, defiled.

Damn, I lost my wallet
To chickity China the Chinese chicken
Not on your budget
Highlighters in a Bourne series book…
Defiled.

Miley Cyrus, I simply adore you

You have the choice
To express your **voice**
Can shop 'til you drop
For this lil' bunny hop.

Wesley Crusher oh where art thou

I love you. Forsythia ever-(Evan clayed
Play with my thigh.

St. John's Wort

Sumatran tea
Ambidexterity
Why, oh why me?
Wax me on, wax off
Brownie cookie crumbler
Makes me see
Me, oh my, oh.

Dwindles down to…

Sex, drugs, and rock 'n' roll.

Well, at least you could work on all the things that would improve you, Nobue.

Self-improvement is always a constant effort to reach that height that is attainable if you keep at it and persevere.

Five years from now,
I will be...

More assured of myself,
Feel empowered by the fact I turned my life around.
Be proud of my accomplishments;
Dismayed at how much I could more have accomplished.
Keep the accolades as a "feather in my cap."

The birds didn't go south for winter

I think I'm attached to
Birds and their own personalities.
I dress like an African gray…
In my grey v neck t shirt
That I wear a lot of the time.
I love sporting peacock turquoise
With an elaborate array of my wardrobe.
I enjoy magpies wherever they're found in the wild.
I enjoy owls too.

Super Power

Seize the day with
My super power
Upon awakening this Wednesday,
I am psychic and can predict the future.
I will use this power to nurture.
Invisibility is an innate ability I'd
Like to have to people watch and travel
To faraway places with no plan set aside.

Growing up...

I wanted to be a primatologist.
A monkey scientist.
Study the great apes and monkeys.
I visited the museum's "Gorillas
In the Mist" exhibit.
Diane Fossey was my childhood hero.
I looked up to her and Jane Goodall.
Jane Goodall's a fantastic individual
Who is great at her study and work with
Primates.

My childhood desk

...Reminds me of the earthquakes of Japan.
How I would hover underneath it in such times.
But I was mostly asleep the two major earthquakes
I experienced. Heavy sleeper, I suppose.

Wonder Struck

Like a gold aspen leaf
Necklace my nana gave
Me as a present
I wore it with pride
To reminisce a time spent
In the Maroon Bells
Surrounded by aspen
Trees.

Sonnet Lacking Definition

Back in the day
I used to say
"Don't let your life pass away."
I let mine pass me by
With lots of excuses and no reason why.

When Things Look Up II

Can't seem to smile today.
I have all the time in the world
To play.
You made me a ham sandwich
Like on a crusade.

When Things Look Up

Don't be downtrodden, okay
You've been thoughtful along the way
I entice you sweet emotes
I like that you gloat
But I don't like you to smoke
But I cope with my smoke
Loving, kindness, compassion, wise
I just wanna say you're incredible
Inside
Inside and out without a doubt
I try to ultimately gain
Your respect when I pout.

Jaded Unconsecrated Lament

How about a simple hi
Instead you're high
Lamenting over my shallow life
Consecrated with lots of strife
Can't put words together in a way
Have lots to say but I'm glad
You're okay
My mind can't seem to unwind
How I love the fact you're kind
Needless to say I am with you
Needless to say I agree with
Your point of view.

Sunny D splendor domini

Holiday Hayday
Too old to collect
Orangina bottle caps
To embellish a binder
Oh how I miss the
Delight.

Cow in French

Hobble over to the aircraft
Southwest solved the Jetsons
Dilemma of the Jetson's mobile
Not having a pronounced name
It's better trying to pronounce
Cow in French.

Could Woulda Shoulda

I could take glucosamine
Woulda done my legs good
Shoulda spent on
Journaling. Maybe
A portion could've, would've
Sincerely should've gone
Toward a car ride.

Just like my former writings

Please send forth my
Articles possessed;
Associated Content.
My heart's request.
I'd been not fully dressed
Relenting how to address.
My life's work.
My mess.

And there she was

Unshuddering see-thru
Days watching *The View*
Compelling outfits on
The women who are well versed
How dare you mock my purse.

Wondering What I might've been in magenta

Can't muster swallow, Mountain Peak
Bashful alprazolam won't go down
Nothin' but a frown
Miss me now? In an
Unpleasant gown?

It being Autumn Equinox, Two girls in Easter attire

See to saunter
Merry go round
Lust has a way
Of making…
In the kitchen
Along this cabinet.
Aligned to be
Possessed by the
Man in uniform
Astound, renown, above the ground.

USS Arizona

You never took the time of day
Waiting for something to unfurl
And be undone.
"We don't have a prescription
For that."
And the sad thing is her shell
Waiting for an embrace of
What has yet is to come.
You parade around and say
Kingdom come.
Now were unwater purified
To be unsung
The last gallows of the West.

Woven in Time

Rosemary chicken
You undo my breast
Knelt a stain roller
A pie
Mag pied.

Lump Sum Debauchery

Write a blank check over
Me;
Oh altruistic debauchery
Have a splendid tea
For thee.

High Hopes for Restitution

I see the bottom of this
Coffee cup,
This resolve,
This restitution,
This ramification,
Isn't a form of British comedy
It isn't me.

Tyra Banks

I bestowed you a
Maundy Wednesday
Barbie's shoes in Yankee candle
Jar
Konrad is Norwegian-German
Tuna casserole.

Heidi Klum

You don't have to say take three on me
You share a birthday with Marilyn Monroe
I was not allowed not to be made in Germany
I have an eyeliner sharp to settle down and prove it to you
You read my mind
America's Got Talent
Fraulein's the devil's candy
Victoria's Angel food cake.

Nick Jonas

The only thing that
Kept me going through
Working at the 24-hour Walgreens pharmacy
During flu vaccine season
Is the overnight
Pharmacist, Dawn purchasing
A 2009 Jonas brothers calendar
For use of scheduling
Shifts in the pharmacy
And pharmacy utilization
And it was on clearance
But meant a lot to us in the Rx.

Opa's Growler

You come utterly defenseless
There is no act to be
Upheld; for let me remind
You if your opa doesn't
Necessarily come back and
Transect in the fifth
Dimension almost angelically
We don't need to manipulate
The earth for the people
Both attuned to soggy-
Bottom boys
It's the IB program; Opa's growler.

UT annunciaretur

Lock the door and
Listen to the music
What?
Without providing details
Latin—to be announced.

Galileo gazes at the Orion's Belt

English to Latin translation
Availability:
G gazes at Taurus
Would not be good
G gazes at Fox Nebula
Would not be good
G gazes at Cancer
Would not be good
G gazes at Milky Way
…is obscure.

Amplius petere vota

A slice of American cheese
Placed in the middle section
Of the minivan driven by
Who would be the millennial
Cusp year, valedictorian;
His sister with brazen red
Unruly lack of frizz controlled
Hair in a dry climate was
Instructed to leave it to
Mold in the side cubby.
The drive me to my destination.
And I am released.
Moldy cheese experiment as a
Way to show that I'm
Too stuck up to acknowledge
The backing of the bible.
Not necessarily Christianity.
As a result. Attempted
In an incarceration in a form of
Hospitalization. She's the chosen
Valedictorian.
Close brotherly sister and
Characterized as a funny
Minivan mood swing
Was it a Pontiac Caravan?
"Ask for more wishes."

Totally Inevitable Presumption

I had grabbed a *Star Wars*
Novelty collector's glass
Without jelly collector's glass
To negate the Smuckers
Glasses they used to give
With collective upc codes
To have a glass
Then you realize you're
Overworked.
Some Packers fans have
A sense of mercy on the
silent of the lambs Seahawks fan
I owe my lover a new
Navy blue but naturally
Black terry clothed robed
Used to help the struggle
Of the regular hustle and
Bustle. So much anger
That the push and shove
Of the tab circulating
Which is their livelihood.
Do you know of a better
Way?
They're not here to serve
A social purpose.
All in the restoration of
The broken sea glass.
Like false assumptions.

Oedipus Rex Next

Please bless this
A bathtub candle
Oh now the vampire tankersley owl cap sleeve
And wash my sins away oh Heather Grey
Youth and the hour of power
Another day and nothing changed
Have a place set aside into the empty (shelf)
Soap down up and down.

Toledo lighthouse

And then I saw her
Abblett of Winslow
In the dimmed courtyard
How her sumi ink
Artwork revealed
A bestial quality
Of the moonwalk into
The terrace of Santa Fe
Now sit beside
A pelted Akron bride.

For Ginny

& then I saw her
Abblett of Johnstown
In the illuminated courtyard
Her authentic green screen Apple IIc
Reflection but her apple complexion
A bestial quality
Of the car passerby
Of a one-way tour de force
She gathers in her
Hummingbird garden, Toledo.
But alas an ampersand beginning
Of this poem keeps us stand
Apart like a couple Tiki torches.

Redneck Wedding

No, don't you even
Think.
Sorry, I'm here to
Mock our peripherals
I'm on my break
Actually.
Uh. You saw me sell
That Apple earbuds earring
At the Apple Store.
You can name Cam Newton's
and my baby Typhius.

Mariana Trench Depth

I hopefully have Chesnick
Earholes pierced ears.

A Wedding Curse

My cousin, Dmitry got married
Hot-ta-ta
Giving the Caffey children
Sixlets to listen
To Judas Priest as
A form of instruction
Introducing the deprived
To culture *Prosperathon.*

Eyes that disperse sparrows

Intuitive notion like an
Echoing megaphoned K-pop
Song time to boost
Up your paralysis
"Out of your lazy boy."
Read the headlines of
The morning paper
To realize you.
Wretched you.
Apocalyptica embed
Armageddon
Wth richness in your eyes.
A depth sparrows disperse.

Ode to Gingersan

Groomed with the smell of roses, a picadilly dog shampoo. Who knew that dog shampoo could smell so good?
Fresh puppy with a squeezed rear.

Sweet Pea

My mom's medical school friend went to Duke
I'd like to think of him as a hardcore X-Men
With the trade name Sweet Pea.
My mom might've mocked him semisweetly
Because he was a short guy amongst a lot of
Girls back in grade school.
He's missing a hand which was part of the
Undeniable ongoing joke that he'd lose
His hand. Which is no longer funny.
But prosthetic claw replacement.
Moved back to Pennsylvania somewhere
And collects a lot of canned goods.
He's got gaming skills and beat the game
Diablo a few times;
He has the innate ability to travel through
Electricity and electric waves.
He's very knowledgeable and is the brightest
In his class. He adored my grandparents
And for that, he will forevermore be
Sweet Pea.

Unpleasant Cab Drive 1

Had a cab driver take me to Office Depot. He made the ride unpleasant by taking me to Office Depot after the postal office but made an illegal straight drive through light when the lane was clearly marked as the left-turn lane.

When I asked him to stay while I purchase only one item, he said he would stay parked, but he drove off.

Unpleasant Cab Drive 2

When going to a therapy appointment, the driver was late picking me up by ten minutes, and I requested him to take the side streets. Yet he was adamant on taking the highway and almost didn't make the turn to my final destination.

Unpleasant Cab Drive 3

The cab driver drove a handicap van, and the ramp collapsed onto the sidewalk to make it impossible to walk on since it was still upward.

Unpleasant Cab Drive 4

Cab driver was talking on cell and not paying attention to the road, almost missing a turn and moving lanes without signaling.

Unpleasant Cab Drive 5

Driver left me stranded down the street from my destination when I said it was a bit further up the street. Then he already made a different turn than I requested and was claiming I wasn't straightforward with paying, which isn't true. I said I'd pay him when he got me to my apartment, arriving there. Yet he chose to make me walk two blocks down the road from where I was supposed to be.

Unpleasant Cab Drive 6

Driver shut the closing van door on me and didn't apologize.

Afterthoughts

In closing, my name *Nobue* means "faith."
Goal of mine is to get caffeine-addict Etsy off the ground after paying
off my towering medical debt.

Acknowledgments

First, I would like to thank Konrad for recognizing his gift of graphic design (and customizing it to my liking). He's a patient person who can tell how I'm feeling and accepts me for my best and worst. For that I am emotionally attached, and I thrive on calling you my soul mate. I care deeply about us and our limitless future together.

My thanks go to Dean Wolf, who baptized my sister and me as children with both my parents present.

My thanks go to all the teachers that I have had growing up, from grade school through a portion of college. Those I keep in touch with, a heartfelt thanks for introducing the English language and you for being yourself—supportive, kind, and caring.

From the silver lining, look out for those family, friends, and acquaintances who are close and dear to you since you won't know when they are gone.

About the Author

A Nissei *hapa* who is of half Japanese, quarter German, and quarter Austrian descent. She is also considered an Ashkenazi Jew of origin background. When she is working, she enjoys the simple satisfaction of helping others in the community. She has a goal of getting a better financial backbone once she pays back money from her hospitalizations.

She's a patient at Aurora Mental Health and has grown and spread to creatively teach herself a little bit of guitar and ukulele. She has taken advantage of the jewelry classes as a stress relief through AMH.

She was born in Fujisawa-shi, Fujisawa Prefecture, Japan, and moved to the States at the age of five. Japanese was her primary language but quickly converted to ESL. She graduated William C. Hinkley High School with high level academia background, being a part of the International Baccalaureate program, but finished with AP English. She prefers speaking in English but can also read, write, and understand Spanish conversationally. She likes to dabble in artwork, plays piano, and has swimming and diving as her hobbies.

She follows several RSS feeds of Web comics online. If she were to go back in time, she would love to time warp to the '50s! She's a trekkie and likes the denomination, evangelical Presbyterian. She suffers from schizoaffective disorder but, with medication, copes using dialectical behavioral therapy.

CPSIA information can be obtained
at www.ICGtesting.com
Printed in the USA
BVHW072037140521
607265BV00009B/682